Motorcycle
Information
Safety
Systems

NOT JUST ANOTHER
HOW-TO-RIDE BOOK,
BUT HOW TO **THINK**
ABOUT YOUR RIDING

MICHAEL WESLEY

Year of the Book
135 Glen Avenue
Glen Rock, PA 17327

Print ISBN: 978-1-949150-78-0
Ebook ISBN: 978-1-949150-79-7

The information in this book is meant to supplement, not replace, proper motorcycle training. Like any sport involving speed, equipment, balance and environmental factors, motorcycling poses some inherent risk. The author and publisher advise readers to take full responsibility for their safety and know their limits. Before practicing the skills described in this book, be sure that your equipment is well maintained, and do not take risks beyond your level of experience, aptitude, training, and comfort level.

DEDICATION

This book is dedicated to my wonderful wife. You are the most loving, helpful, understanding, kind, and virtuous wife any man could ask for, especially me. Anything of value I've been able to accomplish in my life is because you were always there, willing to support me, no matter what.

TABLE OF CONTENTS

INTRODUCTION

Motorcycling attracts its fair share of interesting characters. There is a range of people more varied than in just about any other endeavor. Moms, dads, young and old, millionaires and vagabonds all ride, and love it.

There are many self-proclaimed experts, too—armchair motorcyclists who never leave the couch—and enough people who think they've "been there and done that" to make you want to throw up. I am not an expert. You've never met me, seen me, or even heard of me. I am a nobody. So what do I know that you don't? Who knows? Maybe nothing.

I have ridden all over the United States. I have ridden through the middle of Manhattan and split lanes in Los Angeles. I've ridden cross-country and commuted. I've done Iron Butt rides and spent hours practicing in parking lots. I've successfully straddled the line between risk and reward in both motorcycling and life and I've tried to understand why. There are certainly people who have ridden further, faster, and better than me. If they write something, I'll read it. I always want to learn, to get better. Call it stacking the odds in my favor. Beyond the basics of riding, this is my take on what adds safety without sacrifice. More reward, less risk.

Motorcycle safety has a lot of variables—road design, protective gear requirements (for both manufacturer and user), road signage, training, tiered licensing (based on the motorcyclist's age, or mileage on the bike, or size of bike), and education. The issues and people that impact your safety on the road are significant and largely out of an individual rider's control.

There are a small number of motorcyclists who have influence on the overall world of motorcycle safety based on their occupation. There are riders who engineer or design roads, and riders who are Department of Transportation (D.O.T.) workers setting up construction zones with the safety of other motorcyclists in mind. There are riders who may test motorcycle helmets, or sell them at a dealership. Certain individuals in some occu-pations can improve your riding safety in some limited aspect. All motorcyclists, though, have an impact, whether good or bad, on other riders. We represent motorcyclists to those around us and, by our actions, we influence their attitudes about motorcyclists. Each of us in some small way can contribute to the safety of all of us.

This book, however, is specifically for the rider. As individuals we have the greatest impact on our own safety. Even if the entire world were arranged to be motorcycle friendly (which it's not—not even close), you would still be the biggest part of your own riding safety.

For an investment of a few minutes and a few dollars, you may gain knowledge that could easily save you from crashing sometime in your riding career. This is an exciting and fun look at motorcycling psychology and strategies used to stay out of trouble.

There are many places to find information about riding. Much of it is basic, redundant, and explained in a variety of understandable ways. This book is not another version of that information. Counter steering, using both brakes, and looking where you want to go have been covered in books, magazines, and motorcycle training programs so well and for so long that if you haven't learned, or at least heard about it, you have either just started with your interest in motorcycling or you have not been looking or listening.

The following chapters contain my personal opinions, based on research, experience, and observation. It is not all-inclusive, nor is it infallible. The information presented is intended to highlight blind spots or areas of weakness in our riding which we may not even be aware of. It may not always make sense to you or correspond to your personal opinion. While sometimes basic, this is not the same "basic" material you've heard a thousand times before. It is an attempt to highlight common gaps that some motorcyclists have and to help motorcyclists recognize and develop skills to minimize or eliminate those shortfalls.

Hazard recognition is an art. The more hazards you recognize and the more you develop ideas and skills to mitigate or eliminate them, the safer you'll be.

This is not an attempt to change your riding style, or what you ride, or how you ride. It is merely meant to suggest ways to improve your riding in small, sometimes almost imperceptible ways to add safety margin.

My view of riding motorcycles is this:

The more things you can imagine going wrong, the more prepared you will be when they actually do.

No one is immune from having an accident, but the more prepared you are for what you encounter, the better your odds will be of completely avoiding—or at least surviving—a collision, while minimizing the damage.

When it comes to other road users, if they MISS you, instead of HIT you, you don't get hurt. Make them miss!

1 | WHAT TO EXPECT

You're riding your motorcycle on a nice day and...

BAM!

It happened just that fast. All in an instant. You're down, hurt, maybe dead. You didn't even see it coming! Of course, that's what the car drivers always say right after they hit us, too. "I didn't see him," or "He came out of nowhere."

Why did it happen? It's always the other guy—the *cage driver*. How many times have we heard that it's not really the motorcycle that's dangerous, it's all the other people?

What if that wasn't really the whole story?

"No, that can't be, because I've seen it for myself," you say. Distracted drivers, drunk, high, young, careless, incompetent, speeding, especially from the next county or nearby state. It's THOSE people.

Nope. It's you. How do I know? Because it used to be me, too.

What am I talking about? You KNOW there are drivers who are going to make mistakes and you KNOW you will lose in a car vs. motorcycle collision. So why aren't you ready for it?

You expect to be seen? You expect to be noticed? KNOW from the start that you will not be seen or even noticed, then ride that ride. The invisible ride. Like the invisible gorilla. If you haven't seen it, watch the "Selective Attention Test" video on YouTube. Spoiler Alert: In this video, college students pass two basketballs around while moving in a circle. Viewers are invited to count how many passes the players wearing white make. In the middle of it all, a person in a gorilla costume walks through, pounds on his chest, then walks out of view. Generally, half the people who see the video don't even notice the gorilla. But this gorilla's appearance wasn't subtle, it wasn't hard to see, and neither are you on your motorcycle. It's not personal. It's psychology.

So that proves it's the other people, right?

Wrong. It's like blaming the rain for making you wet instead of grabbing your umbrella. Who would walk outside in the rain without an umbrella and still be shocked or outraged when they got wet? You intuitively understand that's the nature of rain, and grab your umbrella on the way out. Nobody will say that you'll be completely sheltered with an umbrella, but it's a great tool when it's raining so you don't come back looking like a drowned rat.

What does this have to do with riding motorcycles? It's the idea that there are things we use every day for a variety of purposes that help us get a job done safely and efficiently without getting hurt. A hammer, computer, and stove are all tools we routinely use, some every day.

The motorcycle rider has tools, too. We just don't use them. Instead, we expect to be seen, respected, even feared—and when somebody turns left in front of us we act surprised, indignant. "How could you not see me when I'm right in front of you?!" But it happens all the time. It's the nature of being on a motorcycle on the road.

Here's the problem: nobody likes that they're not noticed. It's not fair. It's not right. It's the other guy's responsibility to yield the right of way, follow the rules of the road, be attentive. All true. Except for one dilemma: *you're* the one who has to pay the price for whatever mistakes the car driver makes. And you know that mistakes will be made. So, if you are so hung up on being RIGHT... then you'll be DEAD.

Your arrogance will kill you. Your sense of fairness will cause you to stubbornly expect the other road users to perform at a competent level, and when they don't, *BAM*. You're done.

It's not fair that you have to think for the other driver and not only anticipate their mistakes but also take corrective action for them. So, this is the choice. Either own their mistakes as your own, or let their mistakes kill you. You can be dead right, or you can own mistakes that shouldn't have been yours... and come home alive and well.

What does that mean? In my mind as it relates to this subject it means: If there's an accident, it's your fault. NO MATTER WHAT, IT'S YOUR FAULT. This is the mindset that frees you to think not about what *should be*, but about what *is*.

You might be angry now. You might be saying, "It's not the way it should be," "It's not fair, or right," or "Where does it end?" It doesn't matter. If it's an honest mistake someone made, it would have happened anyway. If it was carelessness, or a malicious action, it will catch up with the other driver eventually. Or would you rather be injured or killed just to make a point?

So how do we win?

Good question. First, let's define winning. Winning is getting home safely. Period. End of story. It is not about teaching the other guy a lesson, or scaring people, or showing them who's boss. It's about avoiding conflict, collision, and ending the day in the same condition as you started.

If you want to advocate on behalf of motorcyclists, join ABATE or the Motorcycle Riders Foundation. Handle conflicts professionally. Don't antagonize other road users. Sometimes things that are legal or acceptable in certain cases aren't always appropriate and can become the spark that causes an out-of-control fire—one that is often left to others to put out.

Let's look at what tools get us to the end of the ride safely, and what systems or routines we can establish for the best odds for a successful outcome. This is not a "how-to ride" as much as "how to think about your riding."

2 | Systems Work...
Until They Don't

In the beginning there was a rider, a motorcycle, and a burning desire to ride. There was a goal: get on the bike and ride. Clutch, brake, handlebar, throttle. Fifteen minutes later, that burning desire turned into a burned calf. Motorcycle exhausts get pretty hot. Especially if you're wearing shorts.

Most of us in the U.S. have a pretty similar story, it seems. For many, riding bicycles turned into a dream of something bigger that could go further. The idea of exploring the next town, or county, or state led from 1-speed bikes to 10-speed bikes and beyond.

Eventually, if we were fortunate, we had just enough of a support system to allow that first motorcycle to come into our life. Friends or family might have given us some pointers or encouragement and off we went. The world was ours to explore... at least until we realized we didn't have the gear to keep us warm or dry when the sun went down or the clouds came up.

There were always horror stories, too. From the neighbor who wiped out in the rain, to kids crashing dirt bikes. Most stories were vague enough to lack any real impact, but real enough to remind you that everything doesn't always end well.

This began our education. Sometimes harsh, always real, often uncomfortable. Doesn't matter what bike, what year, what state—it was all about the same.

Of course, if you lived in Arizona you learned how to stay hydrated and protected from the sun. If you were in New York City, you learned how to navigate traffic. And in just about every state, you found out that most of what was considered "motorcycle training" (after there was training) was the fairly universal Motorcycle Safety Foundation (MSF) program.

This is our world, at least our world in the United States, where the National Highway Traffic Safety Administration cites more than 4,000 people have become motorcycle fatalities each of the last 14 years.[1]

Think of that for a minute. Over 4,000 of our fellow riders have died each and every year since 2004. That's a huge number. We all think we're different, though. We think we're better, smarter, or luckier. We have to. If we didn't, we couldn't keep riding. But we're mostly not any different. We all generally learned to ride in similar ways and if we were really dedicated, we took the MSF course. Honestly though, by any objective measure we all started street riding very much the same.

Here's the point. What if we upgraded how we think about riding? How about if we challenged some of our assumptions? Nothing earth shattering, just subtle things that could possibly change an outcome? Some motorcyclists have already started to do just that. Throughout the country a variety of riding schools have popped up offering, everything from drag racing instruction, to track days, to police-style riding. What is relevant for you? Who has the answer? If you ride on the street in traffic, anywhere in the country, YOU need to have the answer.

Accidents are all about systems that broke down. Everything in the world operates in a predefined

[1] https://www-fars.nhtsa.dot.gov/Main/index.aspx

way, or a system. You flip the light switch and the light comes on. The system worked—the electric generator made power, which went through the transmission and distribution lines, to your house, allowing electricity to get to the light when you flipped the switch.

Many things had to go right, but the system (like most systems) is reliable to the point that you now expect the light to come on each and every time you flip the switch. One time, 10 times, or 10,000 times.

Until the first time the light doesn't come on... then you just can't believe it. The light bulb must have burned out. The system broke down. As reliable as most systems are, eventually there is bound to be an occasional breakdown.

The road system is like any other system—highly reliable, but occasionally has breakdowns, too. A power outage in town means no traffic lights. There's even a system for that though. If the traffic lights aren't working, the intersection should be treated like a four-way stop, and this replacement system goes on, albeit less efficiently.

The cause of many motorcycle accidents was that the system broke down. Often when a system fails it is due to human error. The people who build aircraft know about human error, which is why they build back-up systems into the aircraft to warn when it may be too close to the ground or a mountaintop, and the pilots don't realize it.

What about the motorcyclist? What happens when the system he's in breaks down? You know exactly what happens... *CRASH*. So, what breaks down and what "back-up" systems are available to you as the rider?

Let's take a very generic example of a motorist (car) pulling out from a side street on your right. If the system works, he yields the right-of-way to you, the biker. You pass by and he pulls out when it's clear. If the system breaks down, he doesn't see you and violates your right-of-way.

Now there are many variables and everyone has a slightly different picture, but the idea is pretty universal. A typical reaction to the car pulling out is to start moving to the left, away from the car.

Once the rider realizes the car is continuing in his direction, most riders will continue on their trajectory toward the oncoming traffic lane, and maybe speed up to try to beat the car.

Other riders may start to slow, but most will ride it out like the coyote trying to beat the train across the track. It's a simple problem. What's the solution?

Well, let's break this down and see. Before you started your ride, did you think through your route? Being on an interstate or freeway is generally safer than smaller roads with side streets. Possibly your routing could have been better.

"Oh, that shouldn't matter," you say. "I have to take side streets to get to the interstate."

Maybe, but if you try to minimize your risk whenever possible, your odds of a collision will go down.

Let's assume this was the best route choice and continue. You saw the car. You looked at the driver. You know he saw you, and he pulled out anyway. I've heard people—even professionals—talk about looking at the driver to discern their intentions. Good luck with that.

I've had conversations for five or ten minutes with people, trying to either give or get information, and it seemed like we were speaking a different language. So you think you can accurately predict the intentions of someone you don't even know by a quick glance? You are wasting your time looking at the driver.

There is also something called *opportunity cost*. If you are looking at the driver, you are giving up the ability to look at other places.

The fastest moving part of a car is the outside of the tire. The quickest way to tell if a car is moving is to observe the outside of the car tire.

Look at the top of the tire. If it is moving, the car is coming.

So then, two good places to start are by assessing your route, and watching the tire instead of the driver. Make yourself believe that the car is going to go, not that it will stay stopped. If you EXPECT the car is going to pull out, you'll already have a plan, so when it does, you'll put the plan to work.

We've started to shift from understanding that systems are reliable, to realizing that systems will sometimes fail. This is the key to not getting dead. Recognize that the systems, for whatever reason, will occasionally fail, and that it's up to us as motorcyclists to have a back-up plan.

We started with the driver pulling out from a side street, so let's continue with that situation. First we recognize the car, watch the tires for movement... is there anything else we can do to put the odds in our favor?

I've found my motorcycle's position on the road, relative to the vehicle that is likely to violate my right-of-way, is a key to success.

Most people will notice if someone is staring at them. I don't know how or why, but we've all experienced that feeling—like a sixth sense of being watched. To take advantage of what seems to be a universal response, I position myself so that my bike is "staring" at the vehicle (*see Figure 1*), typically at an intersection, which is most likely to violate my right-of-way.

Figure 1: "Staring" position on approach.

Figure 2: Reposition for maximum safety.

How long I keep this trajectory depends on the individual situation. I'll still anticipate a right-of-way violation, so I will move to create maximum space between myself and the threat to minimize the danger (*see Figure 2 above*).

This is not an aggressive move, and I don't use my high beam. Much like when someone stares at you from across the room, distance isn't really a factor. By simply positioning my motorcycle in this way I have—at least anecdotally— experienced very few right-of-way violations.

In our generic example, we've thought through our route, monitored car tires for movement, positioned our motorcycle for success, and believed the car was going to pull out in front of us. What to do after this is up to you.

The idea or value of our system is that it is flexible and adaptable to a variety of situations. Every road, intersection, traffic condition, surface condition, and weather condition is highly variable. When a car pulls out in front of me, I'm not surprised. I knew it was going to happen, just not when. The *when* determines how you implement your plan.

Most good plans are implemented before the right-of-way violation has actually happened. A slight adjustment in position or speed is often all that is needed to successfully mitigate a right-of-way violation.

As long as you understand the information that is available to you, in many ways you will become able to see the future before it happens. So much focus is put on "emergency braking" or "quick swerving." In reality, many riders who are extremely proficient at swerving or braking will rarely let a situation unfold to the point that the only chance for a successful outcome depends on the speed at which they can execute an emergency maneuver.

Sometimes a quick stop becomes the best course of action. If a quick stop was appropriate, did you ensure the area behind you was clear? Or did you swerve into the oncoming lane because there was no traffic and that maneuver gave the best margin to safety?

The real message here is to recognize the car *will* pull out in front of you, and it's on you to solve that problem. Tools such as what you look at, how you're positioned, and your attitude will all help to unlock the door to a successful solution. Remember the goal is to return home safely.

How many problems will we need to find solutions for during a ride? Lots. That's all right though, because we have lots of tools to solve them.

We should expect a car will violate our right-of-way at the intersection, we should expect the car behind us will rear-end us, and we should expect to be invisible... so we can get ready.

In the next few chapters, let's challenge our own attitudes and see if we can find room for self-improvement. We'll forget what other people *should* be doing and examine what we can do.

Ultimately, what we choose may sometimes benefit an unworthy, substandard, or inconsiderate road user, but it will always benefit us as riders and our passengers.

3 | To Infinity and Beyond

It's all about what you see. The map our decisions are made from is built upon the information we can see.

If you can see it, you can deal with it. The earlier you can see it, the more options you will have, and as options go up, stress goes down. And, as most people have also experienced, with lower stress you often make better decisions.

It all sounds so obvious.

We've all heard "You go where you look." We almost believe it, too.

Watch most riders in a turn... they're a couple seconds behind where their motorcycle is going.

Even if it's easy to see traffic ahead is slowing or stopped after the turn, our oblivious biker won't notice the traffic is slowed because his view is only a few yards ahead of his bike.

From what I've usually seen, he's slightly surprised, but can easily slow before he has any real issue. No harm, no foul, right? Sure, but eventually you're not going to see something important and it is going to matter.

What's the solution? Easy, just look farther ahead, right?

"I thought I was," or "It feels weird," or "I have to see where I'm going," are some top responses why we don't.

Why are we looking ahead? That's the real question.

If I know why I'm doing something, it helps me understand how I do it.

To me, the best answer is "I look ahead to see the future."

What I see down the road is what I am going to encounter. This is my future. I look to see what's in my future in order to know what I must plan for.

To be clear, I am not staring blankly into the future, I am actively observing my future.

If there is a traffic light, I can plan for all the possibilities that a traffic light presents. If it is a school bus, I can plan for not only what I know is coming—which are flashing red lights on the bus—but also children at the bus stop.

Now the next obvious question is: "How far do I look?"

As Buzz Lightyear says in *Toy Story*... "To infinity and beyond."

As far as I can see, I want to see. The earlier you understand what's in the future, the less urgent your response needs to be. When you can respond calmly in a non-emergency way, your choices become smoother, safer, and generally smaller or less dynamic.

"Slowing down" vs. "emergency braking" is way less likely to cause you (or others around you) issues.

Keep in mind, looking ahead doesn't just mean looking straight ahead. Often views can be gained by creative means. If you can see past curves or trees, or if you can use the landscape and/or topography to evaluate parts of the road, you will be more prepared for what's ahead.

When riding a motorcycle, you have options for lane positioning that yield significantly improved views thanks to just a small change of position. If it's in your future, you want to know what it is. The more you look, the better you'll get at picking out what is relevant to you and your safety.

The next question should be: "How do I know if I'm doing it right?"

The best test to determine whether I'm looking far enough ahead is this: "Am I being surprised?"

If I'm observing my future properly, I should very rarely, if ever, be surprised. This is where it pays to be self-critical. If you can be your own toughest critic, you can improve your discipline and train yourself to look to the future.

When I find myself being surprised even a little, I usually discover that I'm not "eyes up"... so that's what I remind myself. "Eyes up" to see the future. Sure, it's corny, but it doesn't hurt, and it works!

We've all been caught off guard. We've all been surprised. If we look at that as a warning that we're either not prepared or not executing effectively, we can allow ourselves the opportunity to learn and grow. A healthy attitude which recognizes that there's more to learn will become a key to our long-term success.

If you're an airline pilot, you had to take a test. After you passed that test and were qualified, you continued to be evaluated and tested throughout your career—thirty years and thousands of hours of flying, and you still get tested and evaluated. The testing and evaluation never stops.

If you're a licensed motorcyclist you took a test, too. *Once.*

You were observed and evaluated for maybe half an hour? That's it. No one will ever evaluate your riding again.

That's why you must evaluate yourself. Constantly.

How do you do this? You've already started by making sure you're not being surprised. The benefit is that you get to continue to grade yourself, no teacher or instructors required. Always challenge yourself with: "What if?"

"What if that car stops unexpectedly?"

"What if it rains?"

"What if the sun is in my eyes?"

You ask the questions and you grade the answers. If you find a question which you don't have an answer to, congratulations! You just found some new piece of information to learn.

There are many riders who put a strip of electrical tape on their helmet visor to cope better when the sun is in their eyes. Many also carry rain gear in the event it rains.

A lot of people—motorcyclists included—like to ask others for validation that what they're doing is right. It's always nice to have an educated opinion to confirm our own assumptions. The challenge with riding is there is a tremendous variety of opinions... often contradictory.

What to do? First, recognize there are a bunch of opinions. Second, decide whose opinion is most relevant to your situation.

When it comes to motorcycle rider training, there are also a variety of "expert" opinions. Continuing training options beyond just learning how to ride vary from on-road tours, to track days at the race track, to police-style training. All with a different focus. While there is always some benefit to any training that gets you on the bike, never put all your trust in one riding approach or opinion.

You could be the best motorcyclist on the track, but will that translate to the street? Track riding usually doesn't happen at night. Braking on the track is for setting corner speed for a clear, clean, known corner, while using markers for braking. Lines on the track are based on qualifying for speed, or racing.

Certainly though, there is some value in the knowledge gained on the track related to street riding.

To start with, how you position each part of your body while on the motorcycle can change how the motorcycle responds. In a controlled environment like the track, it's easier to establish cause and effect. If you don't already know the value of using your core muscles to stabilize yourself, the track will teach you that. Once on the track it's much easier to see the effect of keeping your arms *loose* instead of "straight and stiff." Good physical technique is extremely valuable and the track is an excellent place to understand what effect you the rider have on your motorcycle chassis.

Another benefit to being on the track is the ability to push limits so that you're never surprised on the street, like the first time you scrape a peg... which could scare you into an accident. The track is also a great place to practice trail braking (which we'll discuss in a minute) to gain further knowledge and understanding.

Experience on the track can help you become a better rider on the street, but it doesn't automatically mean you ARE a safer rider on the street.

What about braking techniques on the track vs. on the street? Are they the same? Different?

Historically, most experts agreed that braking on the street was best done while vertical, prior to turning.

The formal rider training and expert opinion generally agreed street braking would be accomplished by setting the entry speed prior to entering the turn to maximize traction, allow the suspension to stabilize, and allow for a steady or gradual speed increase through the curve. The best line on the street would be based on traction, visibility, and distance to (stay away from) opposing traffic possibly crossing to your side of the road.

Now in some expert circles the tune has changed somewhat. Their opinions, and even some rider training, has moved away from braking only while vertical to trail braking—or in other words, braking while turning, like on the track.

Street riders are still taught to begin braking prior to turning, but in some curriculum, braking no longer needs to be completed prior to the turn. Instead the rider can slowly "trail off" the brakes as the apex of the turn approaches.

There are many reasons the expert opinion has changed, but are they right now? Were they wrong then? From my experience, there are times when I definitely want to trail brake, and times where trail braking seems inappropriate.

As a general guideline, if I need to transition from at or near highway speeds into a turn with a relatively tight radius (especially if I have cars behind me), I will find trail braking helpful. I can set up for the corner with a higher straight-line speed to manage the traffic behind me, instead of slowing excessively in the straight—which typically results in a car tailgating. My line through the curve also has more options. If the radius is not very tight I'll usually find I'm not trail braking. Why? Because if I trail braked through the curve or turn, I'd be far above the speed limit in the straight. Usually, I'll make a small adjustment to lower speed prior to the turn, then maintain or slightly increase my speed through the turn. Every situation is different, but what I've described is normally how it happens for me.

Experts often have a narrow focus. Their opinion makes total sense in the place they hold it. But your riding environment may be substantially different. Your motorcycle may be substantially different, too. Suspension technology has come a long way and some of the technological improvements have allowed for different riding techniques. It is up to you to understand why people with expert credentials have their opinion, but ultimately you must decide for yourself the best techniques to use based on your particular circumstance.

What about police-style training?

It's fun and definitely helpful to improve slow-speed control.

I see it in a way like stunt riding. If you've ever seen a stunt rider pull a wheelie while traveling at

40 or 50 miles per hour, it is impressive. The level of control and skill required are tremendous.

But would I suggest that the stunt rider is a safer rider on the street? No.

Would I view that rider as more likely to avoid a collision based upon their skill? Again, no.

Do police riders have terrific trick riding skill like the stunt riders? Absolutely.

Does that skill level translate into a method for staying out of accidents? In my opinion, not so much.

If you need proof, pull up Google and search "police motorcycle crash" and see how frequently "professional" riders are involved in collisions.

Even though I wouldn't categorize it as life and death, any motorcyclist should be able to perform a basic U-turn without resorting to duck walking. This is not trick riding or stunt riding, or in any way exceptional. If you can't perform a basic U-turn, then spend some time and learn.

Where does that leave us in our quest to evaluate ourselves?

Recognize the strengths of "experts" as well as their weaknesses. If a racer is explaining how his core helps him keep his arms relaxed, you'll want to listen. If a police motorcycle trainer is willing to teach you U-turns, who could be better? But recognize that neither of these "experts" is likely to have much relevant advice about the best way to handle obstacles you might face while riding home over a mountain or through a valley on a dark and rainy night.

Continually seek to mature as a rider. Evaluate what you are doing on the bike and seek objective feedback from the best sources available. Integrate "best practices" or improvements based on your own analysis. Try to find if there is an area of weakness that you have overlooked. Gather as much information as possible, but try to avoid overreliance on the "expert" opinion. Not blindly following prevents you from misapplying a technique or idea you don't fully understand, or isn't appropriate for your situation, and also prevents you from being misled by an "expert" who is really not an expert at all.

If you have lived and ridden in different areas of the country, you'll recognize there are different riding styles. For example, splitting lanes—riding between cars to get through stopped traffic—in California is acceptable, but splitting lanes in Florida will get you a ticket, or maybe even arrested.

That doesn't even address the different riding styles in the rest of the world. When you evaluate your riding, recognize that if your environment changes you must change with it. Maybe it's a small thing, but little things sometimes mean a lot.

Riding in Arizona is different than riding in Pennsylvania. Sounds obvious? Maybe, but have you ever thought about how different your area becomes throughout the year?

Trees, crops, leaves, deer, rain, tourists, school buses, and many other things can be expected during specific times of the year. Crops grow and can restrict vision, trees and bushes that overhang the road and drop berries can make the road surface like ice, and hunting season can drive deer into the streets.

If you lack the vison to recognize what hazards are out there, spend some time on YouTube watching motorcycle crashes. There's almost guaranteed to be one or two that you didn't see coming.

If you think about it, that's quite a resource! You can experience accidents that, until now, you couldn't have even imagined. You can actually see them unfold—a virtual encyclopedia of problems that you can now look for when you're out riding... and because you can see them, you can plan for them!

4 | Ego

A short story about ego.

A middle-aged, greybeard motorcyclist goes to a training class with his 18-year-old daughter. The daughter wants to ride but is understandably nervous. Dad has been riding for years, and to support and protect his daughter, he has decided to go through the training class with her. He wants to make sure nobody misleads or misinforms his little girl.

Near the end of the class, U-turns are taught.

Dad can't quite get it, but the daughter seems to do just fine. He's ridden for years, yet can't seem to perform a maneuver that his rookie daughter pulls off almost effortlessly.

Take a guess at his reaction.

Is he happy that his precious little girl can handle a motorcycle precisely? Is he proud that she can apply what she's been taught to cleanly execute a basic maneuver?

Remember, he only came to this class to protect a person he loves as much as anyone in the world, and to make sure she was taken care of.

So, what's his reaction?

He's MAD! He can't perform the maneuver and now he's angry. He's no longer focused on how proud he is that his daughter is doing great. He's not excited that he achieved his goal of protecting his little girl and making sure she got good training. He's upset that he has somehow been made inferior to his inexperienced daughter. He's insulted. His ego has been bruised.

What's the point? If a guy can have his ego bruised by his own daughter in a training class, what chance do you have as a rider if you intentionally or unintentionally bruise the ego of another biker or car driver?

Answer: No chance.

If you bruise someone's ego, their response is usually anger.

When people are angry and insulted, the response is hardly ever patience and forgiveness. Whether or not the insult is real or imagined, their ego has been hurt. They want to retaliate!

In the case of the greybeard dad, he'll probably just say how the training or instructors lacked some quality or skill... but he will be mild in his rebuke since his daughter did so well.

On the road, there's no opposing force. The insult will be absolute. There is no counter to the insult, no daughter to buffer the response. The bruised ego will now need to re-inflate by "teaching you a lesson," or "letting you know who's boss," or "putting you in your place," or any other retaliation that someone's weak self-esteem may dictate.

My suggestion: avoid anything that could be ego damaging so that you aren't dealing with a maniac trying to prove he's better than you (in some creative and likely dangerous way) in addition to all the road has to offer.

How do we stay out of the cross-hairs of the easily offended?

Think through what you're doing and decide if it could be perceived as aggressive.

Anything that scares people will create anger. If your maneuver is aggressive and might scare another road user, then don't do it.

Notice we're not talking about whether the move was "legal" or not, only if it's aggressive.

If you're smooth, quiet, and operating within the flow of the surrounding area and traffic, you'll most likely be fine. But if your pipes are loud, you're traveling 30 mph faster than surrounding traffic, your high beam is blinding other drivers, you're making perceived unsafe lane changes or passes, or if you drop into the middle of a group motorcycle ride while passing... you're going to have problems.

Make the choice before you leave to be as generous as you can while riding.

Vehicles that have flashing lights and sirens are the only ones who can drive a little wild and not provoke fear and anger.

Everyone understands the ambulance takes priority. We all agree on that. If you're not an ambulance, be patient. Drive with extra margin.

When in doubt, don't.

I like the idea of driving like a chauffeur. You want the ride to be smooth for your client and you would never want to subject that person to a police interrogation because of your driving.

If you were chauffeuring a high-status individual, a road rage incident would be absolutely out of the question. So avoid conflicts at all costs.

Some people will say, "If it's legal, then it's my right to do it." To that I would answer: "Would you be willing to die for it?" How would you feel if an innocent bystander was killed as a result? Is it really worth it? To perform a maneuver that could bruise an ego, cause road rage, and result in an unpredictable event that could change your life FOREVER seems like a bad plan, yet it happens all the time. Don't allow it to happen to you.

A final thought about ego. Keep yours in check.

We all need to believe we are capable and can achieve success. But when that belief is challenged, don't be insulted.

We all have more to learn. We can all do better, even at the height of our accomplishments. Don't let something that surprised you turn to anger. Condition yourself to be situationally aware and if someone does surprise you... then be happy. You've been shown a hole in your awareness that can now be closed up.

5 | Mental Models, Hazards & Threats

Assuming we ride with the correct attitude, what can we specifically do to minimize potential for a crash?

I always disliked ambiguous directions, such as: "Be careful."

I prefer specific, actionable information, such as: "Be careful, the police are running a speed trap on Main Street."

Notice the difference? The original 'be careful' statement didn't help me define the threat... or what to do about it. But the latter one gave me specific information that I could take action upon. In this case, the best action would probably be to avoid Main Street.

My goal is to give you specific, actionable information that you can apply to your riding. This information is my opinion, however. As we discussed previously, many in the motorcycle community who are considered authorities have views that emphasize different aspects of motorcycling, with some being completely contradictory to others. As is always the case with motorcycling, you need to ride 'your ride', realizing that often the correct response for a given circumstance may vary depending on where you are, when you're there, who you're with, and the time of day or year.

Let's define the terms we'll use.

MENTAL MODEL

Most people understand that there are a variety of people moving in vehicles in every direction. These vehicles don't routinely hit each other because we have an established set of rules that we loosely try to follow, such as drive on the right side of the road, and stop if the traffic light turns red. These are *mental models*.

A mental model represents what we expect to see. It is our collective assumption of how things will work. We use mental models constantly to allow us to navigate the world around us.

One challenge is when the mental model doesn't match the actual condition. The time it takes for us to accept our 'new' reality will be how long it takes our mental processes to respond to the change.

Let's take the example of a rider going through a green light at an intersection. The mental model would suggest the cross traffic has a red light (even though we can't see it) and we all know traffic should stop at a red light.

If the mental model is accurate, we wouldn't even need to look at cross traffic as we approached the intersection to travel through the green light. However, we should check that traffic is stopped... to confirm our mental model.

The faster we can determine if our mental model is inaccurate and any cross traffic did not stop, the more options we allow ourselves to avoid a collision. We must always challenge whether our mental model is accurate.

HAZARDS

The environment poses challenges to us also. It is not always apparent until it's too late that, even with no one else around, there are some very challenging hazards your riding environment can throw at you.

Heat: Dehydration will affect your ability to process information and effectively operate your bike. It doesn't take long to dehydrate.

When it's hot outside, most people remove clothing to cool down. (How many motorcycle riders have you seen in shorts and t-shirts?) But if you're riding with exposed skin, you'll actually dehydrate more quickly.

The solutions to combat dehydration are: drink lots of fluids, and take breaks in cool areas.

For the rider, additional actions can include: covering exposed skin, wetting clothing with water to take advantage of evaporative cooling, and using a wet bandana or evaporative cooling vest.

Beyond the obvious advantage of wearing protective clothing in the event of a fall, protective clothing can be used to help modulate your body temperature.

Be aware that if your gear is ventilated, you can dehydrate quickly for the same reasons as people wearing shorts and t-shirts. Ventilated gear can be an excellent option in certain situations (short trips, stop-and-go traffic, etc.), but it does have limitations.

Be on the lookout for any signs of confusion or indecisiveness in yourself when riding in the heat. The first time you even *think* you're getting a little confused or you're "a little off," get to a cool area and drink fluids.

Even if it's not that hot, or you "should have been fine," STOP. Cool off and hydrate. If you're wrong and you weren't really dehydrated, no big deal... you had a little break. But if you were dehydrated, you may have saved your own life, or at the very least improved it.

Cold: The cold is generally less of an issue than the heat. But recognize that you can get very cold very fast if you aren't wearing appropriate gear.

This sounds obvious and maybe it is. Yet the coldest I've ever been when riding was once when it was 60°F... because I didn't have the right gear for the weather conditions.

Decent riding gear (jacket, pants, gloves, and helmet) make all the difference to being safe and comfortable. If it's at or near freezing, ice on the road or in your driveway will ruin your ride. Otherwise, many motorcyclists seem to pack it in when the weather goes below 50°F or so.

Dark: Happens all the time, but we don't think too much about it. Turn on the bike, the headlight comes on, and off we go.

Yet we lose so much information in the dark because we can't see nearly as far. All things being equal, riding at night means riding with less information. And less information means fewer options when making decisions, and that's never a good thing when riding.

Rain: Another common occurrence, though this one scares many riders.

> Generally, when it's raining you still have loads of traction available, assuming you haven't let your tires wear out and that they're set at the correct pressure. The key to riding in the rain is being smooth with your control inputs.

> Reduced traction can actually happen anytime due to oil, road construction, leaves, dirt, or anything else that can get between your tire and the unpolluted road surface.

> Add a little rain to that mix, and it can magnify your loss of traction. Smooth riding, and not being aggressive during starts, stops, or turns will allow for the most margin of safety.

Sun: The same thing that allows us to see can also blind us.

> The sun rises in the east and sets in the west. If our route takes us east while the sun is rising, or west when the sun is setting, that is a hazard. The time for sunrise and sunset changes throughout the year, so the route that was fine in July may put us face to face with the sun next May.

How often have we planned a ride and failed to take the sun's position into account? Don't underestimate the sun's ability to blind you.

We've looked at five hazards now which are caused strictly by the environment. All five happen frequently throughout the continental U.S., if not daily, but do we plan for them?

Do we pack rain gear or add a strip of electrical tape to our helmet's face shield to act as a sun visor? Do we plan our ride to avoid sunrise and sunset? Do we have a heated vest or gloves for the cold, or a bandana and some water for the heat?

These are some ways to mitigate the 'easy' hazards. They aren't hidden, they're not regional, and they're somewhat frequent.

What about some of the more subtle or rare hazards?

Gravel: Depending on what state or part of the country you're in, and how many curvy roads you ride on, this will generally determine how much gravel you'll encounter.

What to do? First, expect it.

I heard someone once describe it as: "Instead of 'corner workers' like at a race track, where the corner worker is there for safety, there were 'gravel in the corner workers'"—folks who made sure every corner you came to on the road was littered with gravel.

If you can see the road through the gravel, stay smooth, stay relaxed, don't fixate on it, and you'll make it through just fine. If you can't see the road through the gravel, you must really try to avoid it, if at all possible.

Animals: Whether alive or dead, animals can be a hazard. If you can safely avoid hitting them that's your best option.

Whether dead or alive, you'll be more likely to avoid an animal if you are looking for them, and you'll be more likely to look for them if you realize they are more active at different times of the year in different parts of the country.

As you notice the activity of certain animals rise, you'll also generally notice more of them are dead on the road. Remember to look for them and you'll be less likely to hit them.

A rule of thumb I heard once was this: If you're going to run over a road kill that you could fit on a dinner plate and eat in one sitting, you'll probably be okay hitting it. If you'd have leftovers, it's probably a really bad idea to hit it. Ideally, you don't want to run over any animal if at all possible.

Rough Road: A cousin to gravel in the road is road construction. This is a hazard that hits you in the third dimension. Most riders think in terms of front, back, left, and right—as in, "the danger is in front of me, behind me, etc." But rough road hits you from the bottom.

Usually road imperfections are handled by the motorcycle's suspension. Sometimes though, the road is so bad—either due to neglect, bridges, milling, (de)construction, or environmental cycles—that the suspension of the average motorcycle becomes over-whelmed. In this case, technique (getting off the seat and using your legs to help the bike's suspension), slowing down, or getting off the road altogether will be good options.

The best option is not to ride on roads that will overwhelm your bike's suspension, unless you are confident that you can compensate with your skills.

Tar Strips: If it's wet, they're slick, and if it's hot, they're probably slicker.

Avoid tar strips if possible. Otherwise be smooth, and don't be aggressive when going over them. Expect to slide a little if you cross them while leaning over.

Trees: Most trees produce leaves and some even produce berries. Sooner or later the leaves and berries drop.

If a tree is near or overhanging the road, its leaves and/or berries will fall on the road. If the leaves get wet, they will be slippery. But when berries hit the road and are mashed into a fine greasy coating, they make wet leaves look like a high-dollar racetrack asphalt.

It's not frequent that you'll see this berry hazard, but it's worth recognizing if it's there.

There are many more hazards. The key is to determine which apply to your specific ride. The more hazards you can imagine potentially encountering, the safer you will be.

THREATS

Threats are imminent danger—situations that require some action to prevent death or injury.

Think of the left-turning car, or the car behind you that isn't stopping when you come to a red light, or anything that means death or injury if you don't change something about the unfolding situation.

You could argue that there is some overlap between hazards and threats. There is. The point is to separate out what you expect to see (your mental model), from what you can reasonably predict based on time of day or year or region (hazards), so that you can make sure you're not so busy coping with things you could have foreseen that you have no brainpower available for something that presents itself as an immediate threat.

We've examined our mental model and some of the hazards that exist. By thinking about your mental model, you can recognize what you think you will see, and by having a clear picture ahead of time, you can quickly pick out if something doesn't match.

Pick out all the details that don't match your model and BELIEVE THEM.

Don't look at something in denial, believing it can't possibly be happening because it doesn't coincide with your mental model.

Hazards are things you should be able to envision before you leave on your ride. For example, you should be able to determine if it will be dark before you arrive at your destination. If you're leaving for a ride at 3:00 A.M., you should already recognize that it is dark and that will be a hazard to you.

Sun, rain, heat, cold, and animals are all predictable hazards that you can account for. If you're prepared with what you anticipate seeing, and what the expected hazards are for this ride, you will be able to monitor your mental model vs. what you actually see, then manage the predicted hazards as they appear... all while still focusing your attention on observing for threats.

Instead of just hopping on the bike and blaming other road users for problems which occur, now you will have a plan, you will have anticipated conditions, and you will have the mental capacity to assess and respond to threats.

6 | Safety Multipliers

We roughly defined our *mental model* by saying "vehicles drive on the right side of the road and stop at red lights," so we know what we expect to see. We also introduced the idea that many hazards we will face are predictable. Now let's get more specific on how to improve our odds of completing each ride successfully.

There are little things that we as riders can do which can turn into safety multipliers—small actions that yield massive results.

My personal favorite (though not a secret), is maintaining a healthy following distance.

Your following distance should not be aggravating to other drivers, but should afford you ample opportunity to slow, swerve, or stop in plenty of time when an obstruction presents itself in the road.

My opinion is that a rider should be able to stop within the area he can *see* to be clear in front of his motorcycle. If instead you rely (as many do) on a shorter following distance *because you know the car in front of you can't instantly stop*, you fail to account for the fact that the car can roll over a road hazard without ever touching it.

For you, when a road hazard makes a sudden appearance from beneath the vehicle in front of you... *Surprise!* You are now down to one move, or it's game over. Hope that move is a good one.

With a healthy following distance and your view placed as far down the road as possible to predict the future, you can allow other tailgating road users to be surprised while still keeping a comfortable margin of safety. This also benefits those behind you since they no longer will have to match the I-got-surprised braking or swerving move.

Another safety multiplier is to train yourself to *always look behind you before you begin braking or turning*.

If you incorporate a mirror check into your braking or turning routine, you allow yourself an excellent opportunity to ensure your own safety. If your mirror check reveals bad news, you at least have an opportunity to manage your speed or trajectory to avoid being hit.

It's an option, and the more options you have, the more likely a successful outcome.

If you've ever watched riders practice emergency braking, or taken a training class where emergency braking was taught, you've most likely seen NO ONE checking their mirrors prior to or even during braking. This is a missed opportunity.

There is a lot of emphasis on attaining proper speed, and on how far you've traveled before stopping. Of course you need to be able to produce an effective emergency stop from the beginning of the ride until the very end. No doubt about that. Your emergency stop could even be the *best in the world*, but if there is something behind you that is not stopping and you DON'T EVEN KNOW IT, you've given up any possible options you might have had.

Sometimes when riders make mistakes it's because we're unfamiliar with our route. While we can't account for every missed turn, we do have the ability to look at a 'street view' on Google Maps to determine what an area, or exit, or intersection will look like before we get there. Knowing what to expect will help you recognize where you are, and that will make your ride smoother.

If you've ridden at night, especially in the country on dark curvy roads, you may have realized you'd be virtually invisible without your taillight.

It's not too difficult to see the glow of your properly functioning taillight when on a dark road at night in your mirrors. Even after you've checked that your lights are working before your ride, keep an eye for that red glow. Lights have to burn out sometime and if it happens on a dark country road, you'll want to know before you become a hood ornament.

If the taillight did burn out, you could put on your hazard lights or a turn signal until you can safely exit the road.

Another trick I use whenever there is a car or truck behind me—whether I'm at the beginning, middle, or end of my journey—is to always make sure my brake light is working. Often, a car or truck bumper behind you can reflect your brake light for an easy operational check, especially at stop lights.

Make sure the brake light goes off, too. Motorcycles have switches that can fail like anything else. If your brake light doesn't turn off, you'll want to know it.

While it's fun to upgrade your motorcycle, before spending resources on upgrading the radio, paint, or chrome, work instead to improve your safety margin.

Improving lighting is always a good option. Buying quality gear is money well spent.

Anything that keeps you warm, dry, cool, or protected will allow you a greater safety margin. Adjusting your motorcycle seat, handlebars, or controls to suit you, and make you more comfortable, also adds to your margin of safety.

Here are some other ideas to incorporate into your thinking:

It's in your best interest not to underestimate the danger. Don't minimize that more 4,000 people die every year as motorcycle fatalities. Ease into it. Ego doesn't keep you alive.

Always pick the smoothest pavement possible. In addition to a smoother ride, you'll be less likely to be thrown off the bike—which can happen in extreme cases.

There are two handlebar grips for a reason. Keep both hands on the handlebars at all times.

Stay away from opposing traffic as much as reasonable during turns, and plan out your line through the curve ahead of time.

Look past curves or through trees to see what's approaching when possible.

Visualize. What do you expect to see? What's going to make you crash?

When approaching an intersection, use the strategy of presentation. You want to be as obvious as possible to discourage any right-of-way violation. As previously stated, my right-of-way violations have been minimized by angling my motorcycle so that it is 'staring' at the vehicle most likely to violate my right-of-way (*see Figures 3 and 4 below*). Anecdotally at least this appears effective.

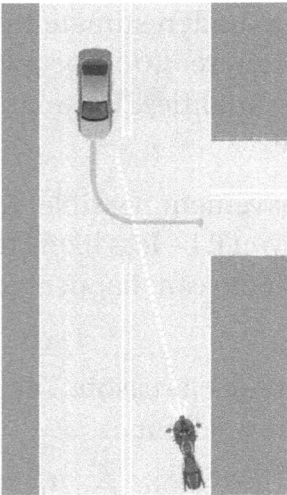

Figure 3: "Staring" position on approach.

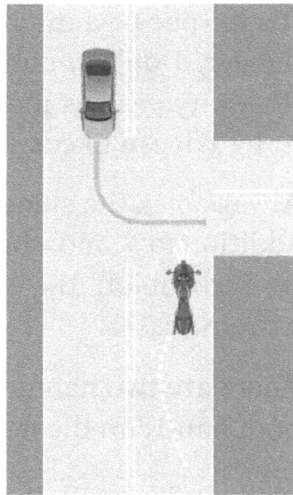

Figure 4: Reposition for maximum safety.

When pulling out from a stop sign and making a left or right turn, where the view is not infinite (for example, where you can't see past a rise in the road), pull out and make your turn, then accelerate smartly. This is a hedge against someone coming over the rise so fast they can't slow down rapidly enough to prevent hitting you. Their only other options, if they can't slow, is to pass you in your lane or go into oncoming traffic.

At its core, motorcycle safety asks this question before the ride: "Are the odds in your favor?" If you feel the odds are not in your favor, either find a way to change the odds, or don't go.

To get to the best answer, ask yourself questions to figure out whether the odds are good that you will have a safe ride. Is it dark? Cold? Are animals more active? Are you familiar with the road? Are you in good health? Do you have the right gear? Do you have training and/or experience that matches the situation? Is there rain? Is there roadwork? Is your motorcycle in good repair?

I use something I call the "rule of three"… if three things aren't going my way, I stop the ride.

For example, if it's dark, that's Hazard #1. Then if it starts raining, that's Hazard #2. Then, if I find I'm going to be in a construction zone, that's Hazard #3 and I'm done.

You can judge for yourself what your threshold is, but that's my "rule of three." Hopefully, I've planned my ride and anticipated what my hazards were going to be. If, however, things aren't going my way, I don't want to force myself into a worse situation.

The overriding message is... *don't get hurt.*

Plan, prepare, strategize, work, and execute each ride like a professional. When it's all over, consider what could have been improved. Incorporate this review into your mental model to make the next ride even better.

Hold yourself accountable for failures—even small ones that went unnoticed by anyone but you. Take responsibility for your safety and for those around you. By being patient with yourself and other road users, each ride will be enjoyable and uneventful.

Correctly manage the hazardous rides, and live to ride another day.

7 | Don't Get Hurt

The core idea is always... *don't get hurt.*

There are two elements to making that idea a reality. The first is a mental approach that consistently keeps you out of danger. The concept of a deliberate, reasoned, and thoughtful approach to motorcycling (as well as some tactical ideas to maintain a safety margin) have been discussed. At the most basic level, if you don't crash, you don't get hurt.

The second part is to dress in gear that will protect you as much as reasonably possible from your environment, up to and including the environment you are in if you do crash. There is usually a level of protective clothing that is appropriate based on the expected hazards, environmental and otherwise. This doesn't mean it's *all* you will need. It just means it's all you *should* need to offer a reasonable level of protection based on the expected hazards.

This is not intended as a "wear a helmet or don't wear a helmet" discussion. All anybody seems to be concerned with, whether it's an accident investigation or a co-worker's story, is "Did you wear a helmet?" Instead, this is a "how can you dress so that you don't get hurt" discussion. Helmets will be part of the discussion, but they are not the only issue.

First things first. What is the hazard?

Am I road racing? Touring? Riding in an empty parking lot? Is it hot and humid? Cold and breezy? Foggy? Raining? Dark?

Lots of questions, right? The next one might be: "How many different pieces of riding gear do I need?"

LOW SPEED/LOW TRAFFIC

Let's start where many of us begin: in an empty parking lot or mostly deserted dead-end street.

Your speeds are low, it's not raining, and it's probably hot and sunny. What's the hazard? Heat, sun, and falling over.

The piece of "gear" that will be most helpful is... *drumroll, please...* water! Hydrate before exposing yourself to the sun and heat. If you're hydrated ahead of time, you'll be more able to make good choices.

From the top down, here are additional suggestions:

Helmet: Obvious, maybe. In this case, a modular helmet that flips up will make drinking fluids easier, will provide a level of protection from the sun's rays when down, and will have a built-in visor for eye protection.

Ventilated jacket: This will help keep air moving. Since you're not riding at high speeds, it won't add much to the risk of dehydration.

Ventilated riding pants: Also a good choice.

Quality motorcycle boots: Boots are maybe the most underrated piece of gear. A good boot makes stabilizing the motorcycle at a stop more comfortable, and controlling the bike when riding easier. Additionally, if you should happen to brush against a hot exhaust pipe—or even worse, fall over—a good boot will offer a great deal of protection to your lower leg, ankle, and foot.

Gloves: Possibly even *more* underrated than boots, good full-finger gloves that completely cover the hand (including the back of the hand) are worth every penny. They can be ventilated too, but fit is the most important aspect. Gloves will protect you from sunburn, road-rash, and much more.

HIGH SPEED/HIGH TRAFFIC

What about an environment with higher speeds or more intense traffic?

Start with your own mental and physical preparation. The best "tool" you have to stay safe is a fully functioning, alert brain.

Hydration and nutrition help you function at peak performance, and don't underestimate rest.

Let's move to gear. From the top I'd choose:

A good modular or flip-up style helmet, or a good full-face helmet: This provides protection for your face, jaw, and mouth as well as your brain.

Recognize that if you were standing on a street corner and fell over, you could die from the impact of your head hitting the ground. Yet no one is advocating that everyone wear helmets when walking around, even though the potential for injury is there.

If I'm riding at 5 or even 10 mph in a parade, I would likely feel okay in something other than a full-face helmet, or maybe no helmet at all, even though the same potential for injury or death exists as when standing on a street corner.

But for any significant speed—let's say over 15 mph—a full helmet, whether modular or full-face, makes sense to me. An added benefit to the full-face version is built-in eye protection in the form of a visor.

One common mistake riders make when not wearing a full-face helmet is using eyeglasses or sunglasses as "eye protection." Unless they are "safety glasses"—glasses specifically designed to protect your eyes from an impact—they are not appropriate. Safety glasses are widely available and are designed to minimize the potential of injury in the event an object strikes them. Regular sunglasses or eyeglasses are not designed as safety glasses. Don't be a test dummy. Having broken glass or plastic extracted from your eye is not an appealing idea. Remember the motto: "Don't get hurt."

Sunscreen (and a caution): Many people use sunscreen to protect against the damaging rays of the sun. But be careful when using sunscreen on your face and then putting on a helmet. Sometimes the fumes released from the sunscreen can cause your eyes to burn and water. Your vison is important, so don't ride with burning, tearing, or crying eyes.

Jacket: Wear something made for motorcycling that fits. Leather is considered the best for abrasion resistance, but is often too hot for summer, and doesn't like to be wet. Synthetic materials work well and can be manufactured to keep you warm, or with ventilation ports to help keep you cool.

It's tough to have a single garment that conquers both extreme heat and extreme cold. Determine what weather you're most likely to encounter and buy suitable gear. If you will ride mainly in the warm weather of the summer, a lighter motorcycle-specific jacket with ventilation will usually work well.

A word of caution about ventilation. When you get hot, your body sweats. When that sweat evaporates, it causes a cooling effect—evaporative cooling. The more you sweat, the more liquid you must take in to replace what you've lost. At some point you will dehydrate if more goes out than in. This is the challenge of ventilated gear.

In extreme heat, another alternative is to wear a wet shirt or cooling vest under your jacket. Then you can control airflow using vents, sleeves, and main zippers to maintain your body temperature, re-wetting your undergarment as it dries out.

Riding pants: Seemingly harder to find than jackets, they are another forgotten garment. Fortunately, from my experience, pants are easier to develop a one-garment-does-all approach. A good pair of motorcycle over-pants—pants that go over your regular clothes—can be used in summer and winter, and often provide some degree of rain protection, too. Unlined pants are the most versatile in the widest range of temperatures.

Protective armor: Both pants and jackets often have the option of protective armor. My opinion is if the garment fits well, that's the key. If it has armor, all the better. If a jacket and pants fit well and the armor will stay in its appropriate place when needed, that is optimal. If the jacket or pants don't fit, the armor won't stay in place anyway so it's pretty much useless.

Gloves and boots: Gloves, like the rest of the gear, should be motorcycle-specific, and most importantly, fit you well. Leather is the best for abrasion resistance, but for most riders a pair of comfortable, versatile, and appropriate gloves for the intended use trumps a one-size-fits-all approach.

For example, leather gloves used for racing are by far the most protective. But they aren't generally good for wet weather and can be uncomfortably warm. If you find a pair of racing gloves you like and have the money to invest, have at it. For some rides, comfortable gloves with a breathable liner may be most appropriate. A glove from a well-known manufacturer that fits you well is going to serve you well. Buy the best gear you can afford that matches the weather conditions you expect.

Boots should also be motorcycle-specific. High quality motorcycle boots for the road seem to do a really good job keeping feet comfortable regardless of outside temperature. In my experience, the high end SIDI boots have been the absolute best boots I've ever worn for riding, and worth every penny they cost.

Undergarments: Even though we now have a good idea of what gear we will wear, there is one very overlooked garment that could make or break any longish ride. Wicking underwear that moves moisture away from your body can help reduce chaffing and irritation that can ruin an otherwise splendid ride. The big no-no for moisture elimination has always been cotton. Cotton undergarments, if they get sweaty, will keep your skin moist and therefore susceptible to irritation. They also take a long time to dry. The best undergarments wick moisture away from your skin to keep your skin dry—plus, they also dry out quickly.

Hearing protection: When riding, wind noise will damage your hearing and make you feel tired. Your full-face helmet does not protect your eardrums from wind noise any more than it prevents you from breathing. Wearing hearing protection, usually in the form of earplugs, is a really good idea, if not always a "technically legal" one.

A concern some riders have is not hearing important sounds like a siren when wearing hearing protection. It is a misconception that you can't hear if you're wearing hearing protection. Earplugs simply reduce noise exposure, but do not eliminate all noise.

The volume of an ambulance siren is between 110 and 120 decibels. A typical set of foam style earplugs with a Noise Reduction Rating (NRR) of 32dB will lower the actual level of noise exposure by 12.5dB. This would only reduce the volume of the siren from 110dB down to 97.5dB—easily heard, even above road noise.

If you want to determine the noise reduction of hearing protection, use the formula ([NRR]-7)/2.

Without the constant bombardment of excessive noise on your eardrums, you'll likely find you are more in tune with your environment. You will appreciate the difference after a long ride when your ears aren't ringing and your head isn't humming.

If you worked in an area that had noise levels equivalent to a motorcycle going down the highway at 60 mph there would be a sign stating: "Hearing protection required."

Here's another "common sense" way to think about the situation. When you're driving a car, do you roll down your windows so you can hear better? Do you feel unsafe when the windows are up? Did you shop for a convertible because it would be safer to hear more ambient noise with the top down when driving? Do you worry your car is too well insulated from outside noise, and you may not be able to hear a siren? Have you ever NOT heard a siren?

To my knowledge, no one has ever suggested that a car with a quiet interior is more dangerous than any other car. Why would it be so different for a motorcycle rider? The motorcyclist is out in the open air, not ensconced in a metal cocoon with an air conditioner whirling and radio playing. By wearing earplugs, the rider is simply lowering his noise exposure to a reasonable level.

It's tough to account for every situation, but my experience is that a motorcyclist wearing earplugs can often hear much more of the environment around him than an automobile driver can when the car windows are up—even without the car radio being on.

I like disposable foam-style earplugs that you can buy from the local hardware store in a jumbo pack so you always have some available. Others have had success with custom-made earplugs. Experiment and find what's comfortable for you. Always use hearing protection, even on short rides. Regardless of the style you choose, not damaging your hearing is smart, and wearing earplugs will leave you feeling good at the end of the day instead of exhausted from wind noise.

VARIATIONS

There are many variations of the gear we've briefly described.

Some jacket and pant combinations zip together while others come as a one-piece suit.

Gloves have varying levels of both injury protection and weather protection.

Helmets come in a wide variety of styles, whether modular or full-face with optional sun visors, either available or built-in.

When you look at motorcycle gear, recognize that the price goes up in relation to certain attributes. For example, Arai helmets are some of the most expensive because they are light and have phenomenal build quality. If your rides are performed comfortably in an HJC helmet for a quarter of the price... great. You would gain no advantage by spending extra money on something you don't need. But if you're traveling cross-country, then a lighter weight and higher build quality Arai helmet may be worth far more to you than the few hundred dollars you saved with a less expensive helmet.

Often when you buy gear, you'll find two items that are remarkably similar with very different prices. Unfortunately, if you are uninformed, you may find the reason for the price difference at an inopportune time, like the middle of a rainstorm. Be honest about what is important to you and pay for that. If you're not sure, then read, talk, and seek out answers from informed sources.

People who sell gear generally know what works and why, and they also keep up with the technology in motorcycle gear that is always changing. They also (hopefully) want to build a relationship so that you will come back for your future needs as your riding changes over time.

ANOTHER WORD ABOUT SAFETY

Protective gear, specifically a motorcycle helmet, needs to meet the protective standards set by whatever authority is in charge where it's sold. In the U.S. it's the D.O.T. Other countries have different agencies and standards.

Additionally, there are other standards that are optional. Recognition of products which meet optional criteria are granted by individual private organizations after a product passes that organization's testing requirements. The optional criteria is also periodically updated. This is why every road-legal helmet for sale in the U.S. has a D.O.T. label on it, but not every helmet has a Snell sticker.

Most other motorcycle-specific protective clothing does not need to meet any standard in the U.S. This is not the case, however, in Europe, where motorcycle protective clothing needs to meet certain government requirements. When looking at clothing, recognize that some protective gear—specifically items for the European market—will have met or exceeded some testing standard. This information is available to you either through the product literature or labeling. It is an additional tool for you to use in making educated decisions about the capabilities of a piece of protective gear.

Finally, if you are ever unconscious, information about you may be vital. Consider an emergency tag that attaches to your jacket, or an emergency "medical information carrier" that attaches to your helmet.

Many years ago I purchased the "medical emergency data system" and think it's an outstanding idea. It's a small plastic carrier that sticks to the side of your helmet, and contains a form that you fill out with whatever information you choose. In the event of an accident, emergency responders can have access to this information, even if you're unconscious. It's simple, reliable, lasts forever, and is cheap.

For less than $10, it is available at:
http://idformyhelmet.com

8 | WHAT'S NEXT

As a rider, you may have the opinion that since you've been successful and haven't crashed or fallen down for years, most of the information presented here is something you already know or is not applicable to you. If this describes you, it means you have successfully stayed within the "performance envelope" of your motorcycle and the limits of your own personal abilities.

That is a key message for success. Stay within your—and your motorcycle's—limits.

Generally, your limits will be far below that of your motorcycle's. As riders, if we limit our riding to areas we know, in mild weather, at familiar times, we will usually have success. After all, if we follow a standard "procedure" for anything— whether a medical operation, an aircraft flight, or a motorcycle ride—the outcome is generally consistent and predictable.

This describes many motorcyclists who have ridden without incident for years. We stay within a very predictable "envelope" which makes every ride almost a repeat of rides we've done hundreds or thousands of times before.

The checklist would be something like this:

- Weather – sunny, comfortable temperature, no rain in forecast.
- Bike – same or similar bike to the one you've ridden for years.
- Destination – no more than 20-30 miles from home over roads you've been on for years if not decades.
- Success rate – very high odds of a successful ride.

My point is this: If we're old enough and wise enough to stay within our own personal "skill envelope" and our bike's "performance envelope," we have really good odds of success.

The challenge comes when something in our predictable, repeatable, and expected environment changes.

Maybe that's part of what contributes to accidents that seem to happen unexpectedly, to experienced riders who've ridden for years. When events happen that push you beyond your skill level or beyond your motorcycle's capability, you will typically crash. When you are forced outside the envelope by something you didn't expect, you become a victim of your own bias. You made the same or similar ride so many times before that you were convinced the next ride would be the same.

Most of us—if we've been riding in the same area for very long—are familiar with one or two spots where there have been motorcycle fatalities. Typically, crashes occur either where a motorcycle inexplicably failed to negotiate a curve, or because of a right-of-way violation at an intersection.

Sometimes we riders take our motorcycles through the crash site to try to understand what happened. We ride through the curve or cross the intersection, yet have trouble understanding how the collision or loss of control happened.

Other times, after the crash, the solution or correct action seems obvious. In hindsight the answers are often very clear. That is the benefit to thinking through and examining what actually happened.

Educating ourselves constantly about the situations we are confronted with, allowing time to examine all the possible actions available to us—and the consequences of those actions—are tools to help us survive similar situations in the future.

Often, reinforced by years of experience, older motorcyclists believe that this ride will be the same as every other ride... but when it isn't, a crash sometimes occurs. Many of these kinds of crashes happen to mature middle-aged riders or older.

To those experienced riders who are accident free, I say congratulations. Keep up the good work—but don't allow your success to bias your thinking that everything will continue to be the same as every other time. Make no assumptions and constantly challenge yourself with "what if" scenarios to keep your mind sharp.

Do not allow yourself to develop a bias that will blind you to potential danger. Use your experience as a building block to higher levels of anticipation and improved perception skills.

A healthy view toward risk management when riding will always be asking, "What's next?" What's the next thing you should be doing? What's the next thing you should be looking for? What's the next thing you could be improving? What's the next way someone can catch you off guard?

You can make a list of "what's next" for both on and off the bike. Your "what's next" list could be related to training, safety gear, or physical health. Anything that keeps you alert to the fact that if you assume every ride is the same, you will bias yourself, and risk every ride being your last.

Lastly, another note about experience. Generally, when we talk about experience, we speak in terms of years. People who want to demonstrate that they have vast experience will often cite how they have been riding since they were kids, usually on dirt bikes. These people are often now nearing middle age and will establish their expertise by stating how they've ridden for 20 years or more.

While there is validity to backing this claim of experience based on number of years, maybe an even more relevant measurement can be made if we equate *experience* with *miles ridden.*

Think about it this way: the average car is driven 12,000 miles per year. If you started driving a car at age 18, in 10 years (in our hypothetical situation) you would have driven 120,000 miles.

The average motorcycle is ridden 3000 miles a year. If you rode your motorcycle for *10 years,* you'd have the same amount of experience as your average 20.5-year-old driver.

It would take *20 years* of riding to equal the driving experience of an average 23-year-old driver. Now, how many 23-year-old drivers would you view as "expert" drivers?

And that's the point. If I'm an *average* motorcyclist who's ridden 20 years, I really am only as experienced as the *average* 23-year-old car driver. Hardly an impressive or inspiring statistic in my view.

While the number of years someone has ridden motorcycle is an indicator of experience, it is only miles on the bike that are actual experience. Don't give yourself or anyone else too much credit for years of experience without factoring in the mileage—to say nothing of the conditions under which those miles were ridden.

We all like to believe we are experienced and competent riders. We use our years of riding as a validation both to others and ourselves that we do actually know what we're doing. Don't create a situation for yourself that causes you to have more confidence than ability.

9 | Focus

We've covered ground mostly on the level of our mental approach to riding as opposed to the physical skills necessary to ride. Both are required, but in my experience, the mental aspects are not stressed nearly as much as the physical.

How do we incorporate those ideas into our riding? Especially in the off season?

My first suggestion is to sit somewhere quiet without distraction, where you can methodically visualize going for a ride. Maybe a short ride around a familiar road. Take your time and look for details and imagine what you might see.

Feel the acceleration of the bike. Picture yourself slowing for corners. Imagine the gravel in the curve (and where you would go). Then picture the U-turn you had to make due to a detour.

If you spend a few minutes visualizing your ride (with real concentration), your riding will improve. If you don't ride year-round due to weather, yet frequently visualize being on the bike, your first ride in spring will be significantly smoother and safer, and you'll also feel like you really haven't been off the bike for long, if at all.

Riding a motorcycle—like many learned skills—is considered a perishable skill. By engaging your mind in an imaginary ride, you reinforce your ability to perform tasks at a proficient level, and in my experience you also improve or at least maintain your body's muscle memory.

A second suggestion for improving your mental approach is this: Take advantage of car rides. There are far more tasks associated with motorcycle riding than driving a car. Obviously, your brain can only process so much information before becoming overloaded or saturated. A car ride, especially if you're a passenger, allows you a more detailed look at the road, the landscape, potential hazards or threats, and escape routes, all with no compromise in safety.

Since most of us don't ride everywhere all the time, we can take these opportunities to improve what we know about the areas where we frequently ride.

If, for example, we frequently exit the interstate at an exit ramp with a decreasing radius turn, with a yield sign and a busy merge at the end, we can take the opportunity to see what view we can gain to see traffic, what speed and line makes sense, and how we can improve that portion of the ride to maintain the highest margin of safety.

The benefit will then also carry over to your car driving.

The only limit to your mental riding is your imagination. Think about rides you've had and rides you'd like to have. Look on Google Maps or whatever mapping program you use to develop a view of the future ride you're planning, and see what you're getting into before you are into it.

Don't worry that this will take the fun out of it. You will never replace a good ride with a street view on a computer.

You may, however, improve your ride when you're actually there because you can relax, since you previously allowed your brain time to process a new environment. Ultimately, you will see more, remember more, and have a better time without the stress of trying to survive in an unfamiliar environment.

Ask yourself: "What is the risk level I'm willing to accept?"

Be honest with yourself and don't let your ego answer for you.

Risk can be very high or minimal. Understanding how significant the risk really is, is a vital skill needed to manage the risk. In other words, the first step in managing risk is to understand how much risk you're taking. And to be clear, when we talk about risk in this context, it means *risk of getting hurt.*

Remember our goal is to get home safely.

So how do you assess the level of risk you're willing to accept?

Think through the ride and what you expect. Do you have the right bike for the conditions? A rider with massive dirt bike skills may be able to ride a Goldwing on a dirt trail, but that would be beyond my personal level of risk tolerance.

What if it rained when the Goldwing was on the dirt road? Risk would rise... so, is the rider's skill level still able to overcome the conditions?

At this point you may have thought there are too many variables that can't all be accounted for. My response is that the majority of rides we take are local, single-day, and not super exotic. So, we should be able to narrow the high-risk aspects of those—whether it's weather (ice, snow, or rain), traffic (trucks, buses, or other motorcyclists), animals (unpredictable deer, snakes, opossum, or dogs), or road conditions (poor design, construction, or slippery road markings).

As our knowledge and experience grows with our methodical evaluation of our riding and environment, we will gain the ability to improve our hazard recognition and assessment for longer multi-day or cross-country rides so that it is not overwhelming, but actually very specific.

Once you train your mind to see what matters to you—the rider—and not become saturated or overloaded, your rides will become both safer and more enjoyable.

A cheap way to gain more understanding of risk and risk level is to spend a few minutes watching motorcycle crashes on YouTube. As we already discussed, there are some accidents you won't see coming, but others you will... and you'll also notice that not everyone was riding poorly.

There are collisions that you will find could have easily been avoided if the rider or driver were just a little more patient.

Other accidents illustrate the fact that going just a few miles per hour slower could significantly improve overall odds of survival.

Still other accidents—even though technically a right-of-way violation by a car driver—could have easily been avoided if the motorcycle rider had been traveling at a slower speed or allowing more safety margin.

Two YouTube videos that made an impact on me are:

1) "My Crash on Mt Lemmon or be alert on ice.wmv"
https://youtu.be/mD3MuL99r9U

2) "(FULL VERSION) Mother releases helmet cam footage of fatal bike accident for safety"
https://youtu.be/hZCadhDW_i0

The Mt. Lemmon video stuck with me because I've ridden where this fellow crashed. The first time, I watched and tried to see if I could pick out what would make him crash, I couldn't.

Yet after studying the video it becomes obvious. The snow melts and the runoff refreezes in the shade. I've been out in similar coolish conditions and was certainly aware of the potential for ice, but not in such a localized spot.

I now ride more aware that temperature can change drastically in the shade, rather than assuming if it's somewhat above freezing, there should be no ice.

The second video is tough to watch. It's difficult to get a sense of actual speed from the video, but it's fair to say the rider was not going slow. Riding style in the U.K. is also somewhat different than the U.S. so the passing may have been more legit than it appears to a U.S. rider.

The big thing that stuck with me was that I had no sense of the car turning until it was already in the bike's path of travel. If you watch closely, the rider had a very fast reaction time. The moment the car crossed the rider's path, he was off the gas and on the brakes. He had excellent physical skill. But it didn't matter. He had no escape plan at the speed he was traveling.

From a side stand sinking into hot asphalt, to being blinded by the sun when heading west at the end of the day, to bending a rim after riding into a pothole that was invisible because it was filled with water... these challenges are all around. The good news is once you are aware of the possible pitfalls, you own the information and it's yours forever.

This is true all the way up the ladder of motorcycle knowledge. It's nice to move from newbie to knowledgeable, but we will never make it all the way up. There's always more to learn.

Riding is physical, but the real challenge is attaining the mental skills so you understand what to do with the physical ones.

10 | Resources

The following are a list of resources I've found interesting and definitely worth a look. While I don't agree 100% with everything contained in these links, that's not unexpected. So, in no particular order, here are resources to peruse.

www.kbikeparts.com/classickbikes.com/ckb.tech/0.ckb.tech.files/fullcontrol/Full_Control.pdf

Free on-line book download from Norway.

bicyclesafe.com

This is written for bicyclists, but there are more than a few good ideas here for motorcyclists, too.

onlinepubs.trb.org/onlinepubs/nchrp/docs/NCHRP20-68A_09-04.pdf

Scan Team Report: "Leading Practices for Motorcycling Safety," September 2011.

Worth a quick scan:

www.shinysideup.co.uk

www.ridesafebacksafe.co.uk

m-gymkhana.com/category/mgx-day-session

www.nam-online.org/documents/Training/ 1211%20Road%20Survival%20Guide%20Final. pdf

www.edam.org.uk/wp-content/uploads/2018/03/Advanced-Rider-Course-logbook-V01.pdf

Interesting and informative article that helps you understand why you can be invisible.

www.johnljerz.com/superduper/tlxdownl oadsiteMAIN/id354.html

Read the synopsis and if you're brave, the PDF version. Not motorcycle specific, but it may give insight to view thinking and riding.

smarter-usa.org/wp-content/uploads/ 2017/05/Deer_Avoidance_Tips_March 2016.pdf

Not all inclusive, but all about deer.

11 | The End...
The Beginning

Hopefully, you have found many things that have been valuable to you. Even one new idea or technique can keep you safer and less likely to get hurt than you were before you knew it.

Motorcycling is a thinking as well as physical endeavor. There is room for fun, frivolity, and at the same time deep study, strategy, and endless ways to improve the experience.

Motorcycling has taught me many life lessons. It is always there as a friend, a dream, an ambition, an adventure, a mountain to climb, or a journey to take. My motorcycle has taken me on many fun escapades. It is my own personal time machine, airplane, and spaceship all rolled into one.

It doesn't matter if it's a small cruiser or a gigantic tourer. I am Captain Mike, setting off on an adventure far away (sometimes mentally, sometimes physically) with a mission of my own choosing. Whether around the block or across the country, the power of the motorcycle is to transport you in a way that cannot be matched or duplicated.

It's also a threat to my very existence. It is a machine that will do whatever I command. Make a mistake or misjudgment or give the wrong signal and the motorcycle will not stop you. We love our bikes, and we assign them an almost magical ability to bring us home safely. But they are just machines. It is up to us to be both mentally and physically prepared to bring our bikes home, not the other way around.

We meet people we would never have met, see places we would never have seen, and experience life as we would never have experienced. The only thing we must do to keep going is... *not get hurt.*

This is the "end" of what I see as common things many motorcyclists miss. After you spend some time thinking, you may find it is only the beginning of the story. Constant assessment of your environment, skills, conditions, and experiences will only improve your judgment, driving you to achieve higher levels of competence, both mentally and physically.

There are many organizations, governments, and individuals that have an influence on our safety as motorcycle riders. Individually though, we as riders have the biggest impact on our own wellbeing. Don't underestimate your own capacity to keep yourself out of harm's way.

Acknowledgments

I'd like to acknowledge all the people who've taught, educated, trained, and written about motorcycles and how to ride them through the years. If you were to list them all by name there would be thousands. It would be impossible for one person to even approach knowing much without the collective knowledge of those who came before us. I'm certain the things I've been taught, either formally through training programs or informally by talking to or reading material from educated and experienced riders, has helped keep me alive.

A special thank you to Ben, June, Tom, and Cindy for reading drafts and providing suggestions.

I'd also like to acknowledge my publisher, Year of the Book, and my editor Demi Stevens for making this idea a reality. Without her dedication, passion, and knowledge this would have remained just an idea, forever. Demi and her team are phenomenal, however, any mistakes, errors, oversights, or omissions in this work are purely my own.

Lastly, I'd like to acknowledge you, the motorcyclist. This activity is not without risk. By seeking to improve your knowledge and skills, you help make motorcycling safer for all.

About the Author

MICHAEL WESLEY loved riding his bicycle from the moment the training wheels came off. The feeling of balancing a two-wheeler for the first time is still one of the best he's ever had.

After a great-grandmother many states away sent a gift subscription for the now defunct *Cycle* magazine, his focus turned to motorcycles. Since this enthusiasm wasn't shared by his family, the motorcycle had to wait.

His first motorcycle was purchased as soon as he could leave base in civilian clothes after enlisting in the U.S. Air Force. He has owned a motorcycle ever since.

Michael holds a B.S. from Embry-Riddle Aeronautical University and now resides in beautiful York County, Pennsylvania, with his family.

www.ingramcontent.com/pod-product-compliance
Lightning Source LLC
Chambersburg PA
CBHW070525030426
42337CB00016B/2110